Riding With The Blues

Behind the Badge at the Sarasota Police Department

JEFF WIDMER

ALLUSION BOOKS

RIDING WITH THE BLUES. Copyright © 2015 by Jeff Widmer. All rights reserved. By payment of the required fees, you have been granted the nonexclusive, nontransferable right to access and read the text of this book. No part of this text may be reproduced, transmitted, decompiled, reverse-engineered or stored in or introduced into any information storage and retrieval system, in any form or by any means, whether electronic or mechanical, now known or hereafter invented, without the express written permission of the author.

Published in the United States in 2015 by Allusion Books, Sarasota, Florida. Allusion Books and the Allusion Books colophon are registered trademarks of
Jeff Widmer.

http://jeffwidmer.com

FIRST U.S. EDITION

ISBN 978-0-9964987-2-2 (print)
ISBN 978-0-9964987-3-9 (e-book)

DEDICATION

For those who serve.

CONTENTS

	Acknowledgments	i
1.	Simulated Fear	1
2.	Across the Great Divide	3
3.	There is No Such Thing as a Victimless Crime	7
4.	Train for the Worst, Hope for the Best	9
5.	Beyond the Gun	11
6.	For K-9 Squad, a Badge and a Bond	13
7.	Damned if You Do, Dead if You Don't	15
8.	Inside the Yellow Tape	18
9.	Not Just a Gun and a Badge	21
10.	Street Fighting Women and Men	23
11.	At the Gun Range, A Cautionary Tale	26
12.	Traffic Stops: the Good, the Bad, the Nightmare	29
13.	With Drug Trade, Big Wheel Keeps on Turnin'	32
14.	Riding with the Blues	36
15.	Behind the Badge	41
	About the Author	43
	Books by Jeff Widmer	44

ACKNOWLEDGMENTS

Many thanks the people at the Sarasota Police Department who shared their expertise for this book: Chief Bernadette DiPino; Deputy Chief Pat Robinson; Public Information Officer Genevieve Judge; Officers Jeff Dunn, Kim Stroud and Bryant Singley, and all of the staff and volunteers who made the department's Citizens' Academy a rewarding experience.

Front cover photo by Officer Jon Vanik, Sarasota Police Department.

1. SIMULATED FEAR

My partner and I sweep into the office building, weapons held in firing position, stomachs bouncing like trampolines. There's an active shooter in the building. People move in and out of the frame, a jumble of corridors and desks, the wounded lying on the floor, workers, police officers, some calling for help. We have no time.

A tall man with shoulders rounding a white polo shirt crosses between several desks and turns into an office. He raises his arm and fires. We edge closer. As the man backs out of the office he spots us and, half-turned, starts to raise his pistol. My partner and I yell "Police! Drop the weapon!" but he doesn't and we fire, hitting him several times. As he goes down, silence crowds the air, and as we inch forward, a dark figure climbs from behind a desk.

Is he a shooter, a victim, a hostage? Is he armed? We've been briefed about the law, how shooting unarmed civilians can land us in jail, how hesitating may get us killed. As the man rises, we have a nanosecond to make a decision.

We freeze. He's too far away to see his eyes but he's got something in his hand, and we're in the open, nothing between us but raw space. Crawling around the side of the desk, crouching in the corridor, the man raises a handgun and starts shooting. We return fire until he collapses. I have no idea if we're hit, just that he's not moving.

The officer behind the computer freezes the frame. On a screen larger than the biggest home theater, crosshairs dot the shooter's chest, marking the places where we've landed rounds. As the adrenalin cools, we come back to a different reality.

In the dim light, everything looks gray, the walls, the carpet, even the screen. We're standing in a classroom on the third floor of the Sarasota Police Department (SPD) in Sarasota, Florida, experiencing the use-of-force simulator as dozens of rookie officers have over the years. Only we're not recruits. We are civilians enrolled in the SPD's Citizens' Academy, a twelve-week program designed to reveal the realities of police work and the people who live in the often closed world behind the badge.

The simulator is a humbling experience. It pinpoints our lack of training and resolve. It highlights the violence of our culture, and the risks that officers and civilians face in any encounter. This is the dark half of policing, the part we see in movies and on TV, always from the spectator side of the camera, the focus on how the situation looks, not how it feels.

As we turn in our weapons and return to class, I recall the shooting of civilians by police in Ferguson, Baltimore, South Carolina. I think back to the first session of the Citizens' Academy and the chief's talk about community policing, the part about cooperation and understanding, about winning the hearts and minds of the citizens, and I wonder how the two halves fit.

2. ACROSS THE GREAT DIVIDE

ONE OF THE FIRST things Bernadette DiPino did when taking over as chief of the Sarasota Police Department was to ban her 161 officers from eating doughnuts while in uniform.

Members of the SPD's Citizens' Academy chuckle at her story but the chief makes a serious point: she wants to counter stereotypes about officers as part of a larger campaign called community policing, a way of building communication and trust with the people SPD serves. That's one of the reasons why twenty-three of us were admitted to the fourth offering of the academy, a twice-yearly boot camp for civilians who want to learn what it's like to work as a police officer. The twelve-week program will cover everything from search and seizure to criminalistics to firearms, with mock shootings and training with live ammunition.

More importantly, it will portray those officers as humans who have to make critical decisions quickly and with little information.

After introducing her command staff, Deputy Chief Pat Robinson and Patrol Operations Chief Kevin Stiff, and our instructor, Training Officer Jeffrey Dunn, DiPino opens with a recitation of her background. As the granddaughter and daughter of police officers, she's a blueblood and proud of it, starting her career in Baltimore County, Maryland, working as a narcotics detective and serving as chief in Ocean City, Maryland, before assuming the position of chief in Sarasota at the end of 2012.

She talks about the challenges of a job in a seasonal resort town as well as her mandate to officers to stay visible, enforce the law and appear professional at all times. Hence the ban on doughnuts. But she spends most of the time discussing her philosophy of community policing. Because officers need cooperative citizens to prevent and solve crime, they need to build trust and relationships with the residents on their beat. Officers need to get out of their cars and answer questions and go door-to-door if necessary to introduce themselves and provide help.

As an example of that outreach, the department held a barbecue in Newtown, a meet-and-greet for residents of the largely black community north of downtown. While initially criticized for the move by a handful of skeptics, DiPino says the strategy has led to more information, more arrests and, more importantly, safer neighborhoods.

My classmates are all for that personal approach. During the break, many talk about why they enrolled. Some want to know what officers do, the policies and procedures they follow to investigate crime. Others want to know how they feel, about their work and community.

Only one of us has experience in law enforcement, a young man who worked security in Europe. The rest of us are here because we're curious. There's the couple who volunteered for the Sarasota County Sheriff's Office, the real estate agent on Siesta Key with a grown daughter in a high-crime area, the wealth advisor with an office down the block whose clients urged him to attend. Two writers, a fine-arts painter, an amateur photographer whose work rivals the pros and a motivational speaker.

And then there's the celebrity. Sitting in the front row is Dick Smothers, a Sarasota resident and one half of the Smothers Brothers, whose "Smothers Brothers Comedy Hour" so outraged CBS that it cancelled the comedy variety show after a two-year run in 1969. That was the height of the Vietnam War and the network expressed concerns about the antiwar, pro-civil rights messages that would creep into the show.

Much of the material was innocuous. Both brothers were musicians, Tom on guitar and Dick on the upright bass. Dick played the straight man and Tom complained of domestic issues, always capping their exchange on sibling rivalry with the declaration that "Mom always like you best."

Forty-five years later, Dick Smothers appears self-deprecating and friendly. During the break, he talks with everyone. Thin as ever, dressed in a red long-sleeved T-shirt under the white department-issued Citizens' Academy polo shirt, he settles easily into the role of class cutup, quick-witted, respectful of authority, ready to praise the police for doing a difficult job. At first it seems odd, the former social rebel now supporting law enforcement. But his appearance has more to do with maturation than irony, a process that applies to many of us in the room.

Break over, it doesn't take long for Dunn as the academy's chief organizer to transition from strategic to tactical. He introduces bicycle patrol Officer Jerry Pucci, who illustrates DiPino's goal of standardizing police uniforms for greater visibility. He reviews dress and patrol uniforms for summer and winter and ticks off the twenty pounds of equipment officers carry on their duty belts: gun (.40 caliber Glock 22), two magazines, handcuff case, TASER, radio and flashlight.

Pucci draws the biggest laugh of the night when he points to a short black cylinder on the back of his belt and announced, "This is my ASP." For the record, ASP is a brand of telescoping baton police can use in close combat.

Despite the laughter, Pucci plays it straight, saying police don't have much cause to use the defensive weapon. "If something goes sideways, I'd rather use the TASER."

3. THERE IS NO SUCH THING AS A VICTIMLESS CRIME

DEMETRI KONSTANTOPOULOS STANDS BEFORE the screen and narrates a list of Florida police officers killed in the line of duty in the last few years. One slide shows a pair of faces, one fresh, one a veteran. One officer leaves behind a pregnant wife, another a wife and three children. The slides continue for a long time. Too long.

On this, the second night of the Sarasota Police Citizens' Academy, Konstantopoulos has a tough lesson to present. He shows a video of a driver opening fire on Ohio police with an automatic weapon after a routine stop for a moving violation. He plays audio of an incident on Martin Luther King Boulevard in Sarasota when crowds and gunfire threaten officers attempting to rescue a man with arterial bleeding.

Konstantopoulos, a sergeant in the Bureau of Criminal Investigation assigned to the Street Crimes Unit, wants us to remember several things. Police work is dangerous. No call is routine. All crimes have consequence. "There is no such thing as a victimless crime."

That theme carries through the presentation by Jude Castro, the victim advocate coordinator for the department, who tends to the needs of people suffering the aftermath of crime.

"The victim advocate speaks up for people who can't," Castro says before outlining the major services she provides, including crisis intervention, death notification and bereavement support. She also helps victims file restraining orders and accompanies them to medical, legal and judicial proceedings.

If you think her job is any less stressful than that of sworn officers, consider that one of her most recent duties was to notify the family of a man who jumped from the Ringling Bridge, a high arching concrete span that connects mainland Sarasota with some of its barrier islands.

Back to Konstantopoulos. After explaining when officers need a warrant to search a house, vehicle or person, the sergeant introduces the concept of *consensual contact*. It's when a person agrees to a search and there is no evidence of coercion — a fine line to walk in even the best of times.

To demonstrate, Officer Dominic Harris and Dick Smothers create a scenario where Harris plays a drug dealer hanging on the street and Smothers an officer who does not have probable cause to search Harris but wants him to consent to a pat-down. After about five seconds of street patois Harris says, "Man, you hassling me 'cause I'm black?" Things go sideways fast. Officer Jeff Dunn, who organizes the academy, steps in to show how police would handle the request. He obtains consent . . . and finds a handgun.

Police work is dangerous. No encounter is routine. Crime makes victims of everyone.

It's a tough lesson.

4. TRAIN FOR THE WORST, HOPE FOR THE BEST

SGT. DANIEL WEINSBERG TRAINS by watching footage of the Democratic National Convention in Chicago. Sgt. Bryan Graham practices by building bombs with Play-Doh instead of C-4. Officer Tammy Featherstone role-plays a scenario where she's talking to a suicidal veteran with traumatic brain injury.

When they aren't training, they're confronting protesters, removing explosive devices and rescuing hostages, always dealing with a high level of danger, to the public and themselves. They accept the risks and seem to enjoy their work. Just another day at the office for three specialized units of the Sarasota Police Department—Emergency Response, Explosive Materials and Crisis Negotiation. The three team leaders brought their equipment and expertise to the Citizens' Academy in the third of twelve classes that give civilians a glimpse of life behind the badge.

First up, Sgt. Weinsberg, team leader for the department's contingent on the Sarasota County Sheriff's Office Emergency Response Team. The ERT deploys during times of emergency or crisis when there is a high probability of criminal or civil unrest. Think hurricanes, riots and, yes, weapons of mass destruction. It consists of three teams from the sheriff's office and one from the city, ten officers per team.

Viewers who watched protests against the World Trade Organization in Seattle will remember cordons of police with body armor called turtle gear wading into the crowds. "That's what we don't do," Weinsberg said. The ERT doesn't even suit up if it isn't necessary to preserving life because that image alone can trigger a backlash.

Many of the drills involve learning how to not to respond when provoked. "As one of our training sergeants said, 'you don't want to be on TV.'"

As leader of the Explosive Materials Unit, or bomb squad, Sgt. Graham and team have a different but equally perilous situation to defuse. They use a host of equipment, from protective suits that weigh 90 lbs. to the Remotec ANDROS F6A robot. It has a telescoping camera, a claw to position an X-ray device and the ability to climb stairs.

The team's primary job is to remove the bomb to a remote location and detonate it, often with a charge of highly pressurized water. No *Danger UXB* guesswork about which wires to cut first. But in the end, someone has to get close to the explosive device . . . if only to pick up the pieces for FBI analysis.

Officer Tammy Featherstone, a member of the Crisis Negotiation Unit, deals with another kind of danger—threats to the lives of hostages and potential suicide victims. The unit deploys two negotiators to every incident. The first talks to the suspect, the second takes notes and feeds that information to intelligence officers.

Her goal is a peaceful end to the situation. "We want to bring everyone home."

A sentiment shared by the sergeants as well.

5. BEYOND THE GUN

DET. DWAYNE SHELLHAMMER HOISTS a ballistic shield and vest and talks about the training and judgment needed to serve on the Sarasota Police Department's SWAT team. He lists the other equipment used by team members, the less-lethal stun grenades, CS (tear) gas and sponge bullets. Only near the end of his presentation does he pick up an M4 assault rifle, one of the few deadly weapons in the team's arsenal.

Make no mistake, SPD officers adhere to what they call the Priority of Life Model: protect the victims, hostages, bystanders and police first. Suspects come last, and if it takes an assault to serve a warrant on a felon with guns, the SWAT team is ready. But all of that militaristic equipment is designed to defend the public, not assail it.

"What about the militarization of the police—how do you feel about that?" Shellhammer asks during a session of the SPD's Citizens' Academy. One woman says it makes her a little afraid. Others want the police to have the same weapons and training as the assailants. Or better.

"The key," says SPD training Officer Jeff Dunn, a SWAT team member who organized the course, "is having the training to know when to use these tools."

That ethic applies to the department's Underwater Search & Recovery Team as well. The Dive Team uses boats, lift bags, sonar, dry suits and metal detectors to raise derelict boats and find weapons and bodies. But the mission isn't about the tools.

"Why do we need all this equipment?" Officer Trip Schwenk asks. "Underwater is a deadly environment. The equipment keeps us safe and enables us to find what we're looking for."

Beyond that, the Dive Team's work can help people cope with tragedy. "It's finding the victim quickly and getting them back to their family that's important," Schwenk says. "I love catching crooks, but if I have somebody's that's hurting and we can give them closure, I get more satisfaction out of that."

On the fourth night of SPD's Citizens' Academy, Shellhammer, Schwenk and Dunn do more than itemize the equipment and training needed to do their jobs. They demonstrate the issues police officers face and the strategy and restraint needed to resolve them.

Or as Shellhammer puts it, "We're not a bunch of guys running around with guns."

6. FOR K-9 SQUAD, A BADGE AND A BOND

IT IS BITE-TRAINING night at the Sarasota Police Department and Bronson looks ready.

The German shepherd remains in constant motion. In the dimly lighted garage beneath the department's headquarters, Bronson sweeps the base of four storage units and finally paws at one. He will drill this over and over, this and other search and rescue tasks, for more than 480 hours of training. But tonight, he's after a big, sweaty suspect who's hiding inside.

The suspect is no ordinary person. It's Sgt. Michael McHale, head of the SPD's K-9 unit, the guy who bought Bronson from his European breeder, someone Bronson should know on sight. The dog acts as if he doesn't, tearing into McHale's padded sleeve as the sergeant comes out of the unit, yelling and spinning away from the animal. Bronson grabs the sleeve and holds until his handler, Officer Jake Nelson, allows a release.

It is night five of the SPD's Citizens' Academy and McHale is explaining that officers only send the dogs if a suspect repeatedly disobeys police commands. "This isn't the 1960s. We don't use dogs for crowd control."

The dogs are domesticated. "You have such a bond with these

animals," McHale says. "They are really a partner. The dog lives at home with us. At work he's all business. When he walks through that door at home, he's the family pet."

They also are used to promote goodwill. "In our program, I want my dogs to be social. We go to nursing homes and senior centers and elementary schools. Three-quarters of the job is showing the public that they are not attack dogs."

Once a suspect has been apprehended and charged, the job of law enforcement shifts to the state attorney's office, the Florida equivalent of the office of the district attorney or commonwealth attorney. In the 12th judicial district, which encompasses Sarasota, Manatee and DeSoto counties, those cases go to Ed Brodsky and his team of 75 prosecutors.

A board certified criminal trial attorney 23 years in the state attorney's office, Brodsky says his office handles 45,000 misdemeanor and felony cases a year. In Sarasota County in 2014, that workload resulted in 131 felony jury trails, 83 misdemeanor trials and 53 juvenile bench trials.

The nature of the work also led to the development of specialized prosecutors. The office now has units for violent crimes, white collar crimes and animal abuse. Those three join the existing child sex crimes unit.

Brodsky says that while he enjoys prosecuting the bad guys, he likes aiding the good guys even more. "There's nothing more exciting than helping victims and bringing justice to them."

7. DAMNED IF YOU DO, DEAD IF YOU DON'T

TONIGHT'S THE NIGHT WE'RE either going to shoot someone or die. And that makes some of us nervous.

The subject in the SPD's Citizens' Academy is one of the most timely and controversial in all of law enforcement—the use of force by officers. To give us an idea of the challenges they face, SPD will run us through the Use of Force Simulator, the same one used by rookie officers to test their decision making under fire. The simulator will show whether we can make sound, split-second decisions without violating the law or allowing a suspect to escape. Or getting killed.

Before we start, Officer Jeff Dunn, who organizes the class, reviews law and policy regarding the use of force and ends with a caution: "When you feel adrenal stress, you don't make the same decisions you would make in a calm, safe setting. It's like everything closes around you."

Dunn should know. He's a member of the SWAT team and a former K-9 unit officer who has faced these situations in the field. If an experienced officer reacts that way, how will that stress affect us?

We find out quickly. The class enters the simulator four at a time. My group consists of Barna, Tracy, Bill and me. Barna worked security in Europe so he's used to some of this. The rest of us look like the civilians we are.

The theater-like simulator consists of a computer, projector and life-size screen that plays an interactive video. Officer Kim Stroud conducts the drill, showing us how to hold our weapons, enter a building and communicate with our partner. The Glock and the TASER™ are real, the bullets and prongs replaced with lasers that not only target suspects but display the accuracy of our fire.

In the first scenario, Bill and I respond to an active-shooter situation in an office building. Dispatch has no other information. Armed with guns, Bill and I simulate walking down hallways past bodies of workers and officers. We turn a corner and hear shots and a man in a white shirt walks into a room and starts firing.

Bill yells "Sarasota Police!" and as the suspect backs out of the office we fire. Just as the man goes down, another pops up from behind a desk and, before we can get off a round, shoots at us. We fire back and, as he clears the desk, we finally bring him down. Stroud replays parts of the exchange. The computer shows crosshatch marks where our bullets hit. The desk is a goner but we didn't hit the shooter until he'd squeezed off several rounds. I don't know how many, it happens so fast.

In the second scenario, Bill holds the Glock and I hold a TASER. We're called to a disturbance and find a woman fighting with an officer on the street. As she grows more violent, the officer moves off and the suspect screams and waves something in her right hand. The use of potentially lethal force is not needed so I yell "TASER! TASER! TASER!" and pull the trigger. The devices crackles and the woman hits the concrete.

Stroud looks as if I've waited too long. She's probably right.

In their first scenario, Tracy and Barna respond to a reported break-in at an office building after hours. No other information is available, so they go in blind. Tracy holds the TASER, Barna the Glock. As they move through the building, they see a man sitting at a desk. He looks calm and talks to them. Suddenly he stands and raises what looks like a weapon. The pair fire, Barna hitting the suspect in the foot and knee. Tracy brings him down, landing the TASER prongs over the guy's heart. The assailant's weapon turns out to be a stapler.

In the second scenario, Tracy and Barna respond to a domestic dispute. They weave their way through a warren of halls to confront a person yelling at a man who's seated in front of a fireplace. He's holding a shotgun between his legs. Before either officer can react, the assailant tilts the gun slightly and fires. As the screen goes blank, Barna fires his weapon.

Stroud pushes back from the computer and says what officers must hope they'll never hear. "Too late."

8. INSIDE THE YELLOW TAPE

The phone rings at 2 a.m. Dispatch reports two unresponsive adults in a car in a parking garage next to Kari's Restaurant. Officers have secured the scene. Detectives from the Criminal Investigation Division, or CID, are on the way. As part of the Criminalistics Unit, so are we.

Our team walks into the parking garage to find a gold Prius encircled in yellow crime-scene tape, a bottle of Corona a few feet from the car, liquid splashing the concrete. On the deck, a plastic sandwich bag and what looks like a candy wrapper.

In the front seats, a man and woman in their late twenties or early thirties, the driver holding a gun. He's wearing a black short-sleeved athletic shirt, black pants, ring, no watch. He's been shot once in the right temple. She's wearing a white short-sleeved shirt with khaki pants, a ring and a watch. She's been shot once in the left temple.

A shell casing rests on the dash, another on the back seat, a Super Vel .44 Mag. Two bottles of insect repellant in the seat pocket. Papers in the trunk.

As we crawl around the car, the lead technician, Kari McVaugh, says, "Don't get tunnel vision. Don't get focused on the yellow tape."

So begins the scenario created by the Sarasota Police Department for week seven of its Citizens' Academy, the program that runs residents through the same training as police officers. The bodies in the car are real, officers playing roles that allow us to collect and analyze evidence like our civilian counterparts in the real Criminalistics Unit.

Back in the classroom, we review surveillance footage from the garage and video of two interviews with the department's prime suspect, the owner of Kari's bar, played with magnificent realism by McVaugh. As we watch, Sgt. Tom Shanafelt of the department's Major Crimes Unit tell us what to observe, what to doubt and what would happen if we worked in CID.

We would run the tag and compare a license photo with the deceased—turns out he's Kari's ex-husband. Surveillance video shows Kari helping both victims to the car and then wiping her hands on a towel as she walks away. We would ask experts to analyze body fluids, fluids on the towel, tool markings on the shell casings.

Months later during a second interview, two detectives have suspect Kari wedged in a corner of a bare interrogation room. The first thing they do is read her Miranda rights. Then they present DNA evidence that contradicts her initial statement and press her about her mental state. She's confrontational at first, sticking to her story, telling detectives her medical history is none of their business. She backs up, fidgets, stares at her hands. She's confused. She doesn't understand why the DNA evidence should matter.

Finally, she confesses, ending her monologue with, "I guess I just snapped." Detectives charge and cuff her.

While the confession solves the case, the collection and analysis of evidence wins it, every careful step from autopsy to interview. Or as Shanafelt puts it, "The next-best thing to a confession is a provable lie."

9. NOT JUST A GUN AND A BADGE

"POLICE OFFICERS ARE HUMAN," Training Officer Jeffrey Dunn tells members of the SPD Citizens' Academy. "Some of them do stupid things sometimes."

And some of them do good and brave things. Genevieve Judge, the department's public information officer, wants to get both of those messages to the media and the public. She knows that a fast, honest response to a negative situation can build trust. And that publicizing the positive things officers do can help build understanding and goodwill, something that seems in short supply these days.

"There are good police officers and there are bad police officers," Judge says. "It's how you handle the situation that people will remember. We can ignore it or we can stay in front of it. Even if we're not proud of it, I'd rather people hear about it from us so they get the whole story."

To that end, Judge, a veteran television reporter and videographer, launched the department into the world of social sharing when she came on board in 2013, creating a dialog with residents on the major networks. With the backing of Chief Bernadette DiPino, she routinely posts on Facebook, Twitter

(@SarasotaPD), YouTube and Instagram.

Judge covers all major public events, does ride-alongs with officers called Tweet from the Beat and shoots video for initiatives like Click It or Ticket and Shop with a Cop, a program for children that runs around the holidays. She also fields questions and requests for arrest reports from journalists who are also trying to balance coverage, often pitting citizens against the police and putting the department on the defense.

Like the academy itself, the social media feed gives residents a behind-the-scenes look at the department and its personnel. It helps them balance the news they see and hear from other sources. "I want people to see it on our social networks before they see it anywhere else," Judge says. "That way we own it and it comes from a trusted source."

The publicity serves another purpose. "It shows our officers are not just a gun and a badge. They are human."

No one knows that better than Jeff Dunn, who started with the Bradenton Police Department in 1992 and has worked on the K-9, SWAT and field training teams. In addition to organizing the Citizens' Academy, he trains recruits and experienced officers in diversity, firearms, non-lethal weapons and law-enforcement policies and procedures.

"It's not the most dangerous job but it's the most rewarding. In police work, anything that goes wrong comes back to training. We make sure everything is correct and accurate and up to date."

Firing-range practice is essential but training must encompass real-world situations. That's why Dunn uses scenario-based training, creating events that are realistic, such as putting officers in situations that require them to use defensive tactics. "Not many police officers are attacked by paper targets."

There are days when Genevieve Judge must feel the same way.

10. STREET FIGHTING WOMEN AND MEN

THE PATROL CAR DASH-CAM shows officers of the Cottonwood Police Department approaching a family in a Wal-Mart parking lot after midnight on March 21, 2015. The police are responding to an alleged assault of a Wal-Mart employee, a relatively routine call in Arizona, or anywhere else. When officers arrive, they find eight people milling around what looks like a heap of laundry bags behind a Chevrolet Suburban.

As another patrol car arrives, one of the officers says, "We need to separate these folks and talk to them."

"No, you're not going to get . . . you're not going to separate me from my family," a male family member says.

And then they attack, hitting officers, gouging their faces, wrestling for their weapons. Police try pepper spray, TASERs, a baton. Nothing works. The combatants pummel the police. They raise their hands in surrender only to resume the attack. By the time the fight ends, one officer has been shot, one suspect is dead, another wounded and seven in custody. The fight lasts seven minutes.

Later, the *Arizona Republic* will report that the Gaver family performs as musicians on the streets of Boise, Idaho. For the past four days they have been living from their car in the Wal-Mart parking lot in Cottonwood, a town of 11,000 located about 60 miles southwest of Flagstaff.

"It's an example of how things can go wrong fast," Sarasota Police Officer Sean Gleason says as he shows the video to residents in the SPD Citizens' Academy. "I show this video to the [members of the police] defensive tactics class because we need to know about fighting. I want [the officers] to say, 'I'd survive this situation.'"

The situations are becoming more common. "These days, everybody knows this stuff. They see martial arts on TV all the time. You could be doing a routine traffic stop and the next thing you know you're fighting for your life."

Which is why the department's lead defensive-tactics instructor teaches Brazilian jujitsu, a ground-fighting martial art that schools officers in grappling techniques and escapes.

The inside of the SPD defensive tactics room looks like my high school wrestling class, with thick blue pads on the walls and floor and a yellow bucket and mop in the corner. Gleason, a K-9 officer, and assistant SWAT team leader Det. Dwayne Shellhammer demonstrate the moves police are most likely to need. Such as when drunks pile out of a bar and start a fight and officers have to wade into the pack.

In that situation, the drunks often turn on the officers. The assailants are so close officers can't draw their weapons. They move too quickly to handcuff. Someone grabs an officer around the throat from behind and pulls. That action shows intent to hurt or kill the officer, and lethal force is justified, but Gleason and Shellhammer know a better way. Gleason breaks the hold and applies pressure to the sides of the neck, explaining the move as he demonstrates it.

"We're the only agency that does the vascular neck restraint. It's a blood choke where you cut the blood flow to the brain. It's not like this." He puts his arm across Shellhammer's throat. "That's a choke hold and it can be lethal. The VNR will put them to sleep." Shellhammer's face glows red, a testament to the effectiveness of the hold.

"When you become a police officer," Gleason says, "you have to completely change the way you think about things . . . everything you do, whether eating dinner or making a traffic stop. You ask yourself, 'what am I going to do if somebody walks in with a gun or someone in that car shoots at me?' Every call you go on, you have to think, 'is this person going to attack me and am I ready?' Mom, dad, a kid . . . anybody could kill you at any time."

11. AT THE GUN RANGE, A CAUTIONARY TALE

AFTER HOURS OF INSTRUCTION, we file onto the gun range and prepare to shoot. Three officers have reviewed the standard-issue weapons of the Sarasota Police Department: a Glock 22 handgun, a Colt AR-15 rifle and a Remington 870 pump shotgun. Today we're going to fire the Glock.

Dressed in our white shirts with the blue SPD Citizens' Academy logo, about fifteen of us line up at the gun range at Knight Trail Park in Nokomis, Florida, to receive eye and ear protection and more instruction. Some classmates have permits to carry guns, although personal weapons are banned today. Some have worked as firearms instructors. I shot a rifle in high school but it was a bolt-action .22. I've never handled a handgun and, until today, never had the desire.

SPD Training Officer Kim Stroud instructs us in how to hold and aim the Glock. The strong hand wraps around the grip, index finger pointing forward, never on the trigger until you're ready to shoot. That prevents accidental firing due to muscle twitch. The supporting hand wraps around the fingers on the grip with the thumb pointing forward. "That's 60 percent of your control."

As I listen, I remember the warning SPD Training Officer Jeff

Dunn gave as soon as we walked into his classroom, the most important of all of the safety rules: Even if the weapon is disassembled or unloaded, "We are never going to point a gun at anything we aren't willing to destroy." Today that includes our fellow classmates.

As she leads us downrange, Stroud repeats that message. The range is built with concrete strips like football field markers starting 50 yards from the targets. Stroud stops at the 3-yard marker, in front of a paper silhouette of a head and torso backed by a sandy hill. Dunn, a member of the SPD SWAT team, flanks her on the right and maintains control of the magazine. Officer Ken Goebel, the former leader of the department's sniper team, stands where he can see us and the shooter.

I step up. Stroud hands the Glock to me and positions my hands. At no time does she let go of the weapon. She places her other hand on my back so the weapon doesn't come up to the 180-degree position after firing.

The target has a red circle in the center of the chest and a smaller one in the middle of the head. As I line up the front and rear sights on the larger circle, the target seems to waver. It's the slight motion of the hands. Stroud says that's normal. She steadies the gun and inserts the magazine. I grip harder, inhale, hold my breath and squeeze the trigger.

Everything happens at once. I hear an explosion, loud but not as loud as a cherry bomb, and the gun kicks up but not far. There's little recoil into the palm. With the ear protection, I don't even hear the clink of the shell as it hits the concrete. The bullet rips through the target and scuffs the bank, kicking up a small plume of sand. I see a small bright hole in the red dot, not dead center but close, slightly below where I've aimed.

We take turns, each firing a single round, then Dunn and

Goebel give a brief demonstration of the rifle and shotgun. I'm reminded of the use-of-force simulator, where you have a nanosecond to decide whether to fire on a suspect. Safety training takes 2½ hours. Our one shot takes 30 seconds at most.

SPD officers receive far more instruction—mandatory training twice a year for all sworn officers with additional rifle training for the patrol unit. These are real-world scenarios that stress shooting while moving while minimizing collateral damage. Officers also practice fixing and reloading their weapon during combat.

Range practice over, the class breaks for lunch. It's Goebel's day off and Dunn has enlisted his help as cook. He grills hamburgers and hot dogs and we sit on picnic tables under a lean-to roof and listen to stories we rarely hear from police, stories about triumphs and mistakes, about devotion and misspent youth.

It is the best part of the day.

12. TRAFFIC STOPS: THE GOOD, THE BAD, THE NIGHTMARE

IT WAS SUPPOSED TO be a routine traffic stop. In March of 2013, two Middlefield, Ohio, police officers pull over a Saturn sedan for running a stop sign. In the video, the sky's a typical washed-out winter blue. Cars keep rolling down the street as if nothing's happening in this town of 2,700, located 45 miles due east of Cleveland.

Suddenly the driver opens his door and unleashes thirty-seven rounds from an AK-47. The patrol car's windshield splinters. Smoke drifts across the dash-cam as the officers return fire. "Kill me!" the man shouts and collapses in the street.

Police had pulled the driver over for a simple moving violation. The stop turned into an armed attack that resulted in the death of the driver and the injury of both officers.

Most traffic stops don't end like that one but the danger exists—witness the killing of two officers in Hattiesburg, Mississippi, on May 9. So does the legal hazard of police violating a citizen's Fourth Amendment right to protection from illegal search and seizure. For the Sarasota Police Department, where three officers face investigation after a man pulled over for a moving violation died, traffic stops are anything but routine.

Officers Helios Blanco and John Vanik show the Middlefield video to members of the SPD Citizens' Academy to make a point: that when it comes to traffic stops, the operative word is safety. Police must protect themselves when approaching a vehicle. Drivers should keep that in mind when evaluating an officer's behavior . . . and their own.

There are three types of traffic stops: routine; redirect, where the stop becomes a criminal investigation; and pretext, where police use a legitimate traffic violation for a closer look at the suspect. Call them the good, the bad and the really ugly, the Middlefield shooter the poster child for the latter.

"Every traffic stop is different—the person, the weather, the location," says Vanik, a patrol division officer who specializes in DUI checks. "When I stop a car, I don't know who's in the car, their race, their nationality, even after I run the tag and make contact. Everybody has tinted windows and when it's two in the morning and it's a dark street, I can't even tell if there's a person in the car."

An officer's first step is to determine the number of occupants and whether they are moving in an effort to hide guns or conceal drugs. After that, police look for signs of trouble. "Bumper stickers are a giveaway. NRA stickers tell me there's a gun in car. Stickers like 'I hate government' and 'I hate police' tell me how they feel.

"Most of the time," Vanik says, "people are polite to us." Still, he and other officers park so they can shine headlights on the suspect's car and use theirs as a shield. They will order suspects out of the vehicle and have them walk backwards. They will stand where a shooter would not expect to find them.

"Always, keep eyes on," says Blanco, a gang officer and

Spanish-speaking translator. "Those few seconds can make the difference between me going home or going to the morgue."

Since 52% of all encounters with police occur during traffic stops, SPD offers this advice:

- When you notice lights behind you, pull your vehicle to the curb and stay stopped.
- Keep both hands on the steering wheel until the officer approaches.
- Provide your license, registration and proof of insurance.
- The officer will tell you the reason for the stop.
- Back in the patrol car, the officer will check DMV records to determine if the vehicle is stolen or if the driver is on inmate release.
- The officer will say whether you will receive a citation or a warning.

If the officer smells something coming from the car, he or she may have probable cause to search the vehicle. "The window is down," Blanco says. "I get an odor. It's not Febreze. If it's marijuana, we have probable cause to search."

Not so with alcohol. Vanik says police need at least two behavioral cues to conduct a field sobriety test, such as the smell of alcohol and the driver's slurred speech.

Regardless of whether the stop results in a warning or something more serious, the encounter is usually stressful for everyone.

"I never say 'have a nice day,'" Blanco says. "I say, 'take care.'"

Good advice . . . for all concerned.

13. WITH DRUG TRADE, BIG WHEEL KEEPS ON TURNING

THE DRIVER WITH THE dreadlocks to his shoulders backs into the parking space at the marina near downtown Sarasota and powers down the window. He's looking to buy 200 oxycodone pills from an undercover agent with the Sarasota Police Department. The agent, a man with graying hair and a shirt slung over his shoulder, leans in to talk.

From a nearby car, members of the SPD narcotics unit who are filming the encounter begin to see red flags. The driver backed in, indicating he's preparing for a fast getaway. He's on the phone. He's flashing a wad of cash with a twenty on top and ones underneath. The deal's worth $1,600, so the buyer intends to steal the drugs. He wants to count the pills and tells the undercover agent to get in the car. The officer refuses.

Before anyone can react, the passenger reaches across the driver and points a handgun at the agent's head. The driver bolts. Officers stop him before he can leave the parking lot.

"We did get him," the sergeant in charge of the unit tells members of the SPD Citizens' Academy. "We had controlled phone calls of their intent to do the deal. That's an attempted armed robbery, and it trumps the drug charge. It was a loaded .45 handgun."

Detectives were seeing an uptick in the abuse of prescription medication like Percocet and OxyContin until local law enforcement, led by the Sarasota County Sheriff's Office, began a crackdown in 2009. Since then, the target has shifted.

"As far as upper-level crime, what we mostly see is cocaine," a detective in the SPD unit says. "We're starting to see a lot more heroin because oxycodone has become more expensive. People are lacing heroin with fentanyl [a synthetic opioid analgesic that is 80 times more potent than morphine] to increase potency. They're dying with the needle in their arm."

But the big drug today is Spice.

The Associated Press is reporting a huge nationwide spike in hospitalizations caused by synthetic marijuana. In early 2015, the number of cases rocketed from 359 in January to more than 1,500 in April, according to the American Association of Poison Control Centers. Synthetic marijuana usually is a non-marijuana plant material sprayed with cannabinoids and marketed under brand names like Spice, K2 and Scooby Snax.

After two people died at Sarasota's New College of Florida in early May of 2015, the Sarasota Police Department said its initial investigation showed that "both deaths appeared to be drug related." The region's medical examiner has labeled the situation an "epidemic."

"This stuff is really bad," the drug-unit sergeant says. "Users don't know what they're smoking. People put potpourri in cement mixers and spray it with chemicals they get from China, Level 1 narcotics like XLR-11 [an ingredient in synthetic cannabis]. That's why these people are going crazy when they smoke it. These chemicals, they're a lethal cocktail."

The SPD narcotics unit consists of five officers and a technician in charge of the recording equipment. The unit does undercover drug buys, executes searches and conducts long-term investigations to nab importers and dealers.

Detectives get their cases from a variety of sources—neighbor complaints, patrol division reports, Crime Stoppers of Sarasota and other hotline programs. They follow prostitutes to drug houses. They do surveillance to verify information. They drive unmarked cars through dealer turf and set up street buys with cameras covering every inch of the car's interior.

One of the most effective tools is the confidential informant. "A lot of times we'll arrest somebody who says he's tired of this life," the sergeant says. "Once we determine that they're fairly mentally capable, we'll pay that person to do a controlled drug buy for us." He pauses and in those few seconds you can watch the wheels turn as he mulls the unanswered questions from the audience, about the Faustian bargain, about ethics rather than souls, so he adds, "We say we're making a deal with the devil," and leaves it at that.

Detectives can take only so much product out of circulation with street-level deals. So they work with federal authorities in the Drug Enforcement Administration and the Bureau of Alcohol, Tobacco, Firearms and Explosives to arrest leaders and escalate charges to levels they hope will sideline suppliers.

In 2014 the unit wrapped up a two-year investigation called SRQ Cartel II that resulted in the arrest of ten people alleged to be mid-level suppliers. Police confiscated twelve kilograms of cocaine, five cars, seven guns and $115,000. A prior sweep resulted in the arrest of a Sarasota man allegedly tied to a Mexican drug cartel.

"Our goal," the sergeant says, "is to climb the ladder."

Publicly, both he and the detective—I'm not naming or photographing them to protect their ability to conduct undercover work—call their job "stressful, dangerous and fun." Privately, while proud of their work to remove the cause of other crimes such as burglary and assault, they have times of doubt.

Such as the day when an informant who promised to go straight climbed into their car for another deal. "The detective pulled his hat down over his face," the sergeant says. "The informant didn't even recognize him."

He shakes his head at the memory. "You put them away and more take their place. Sometimes you feel like a gerbil on a wheel."

14. RIDING WITH THE BLUES

OFFICER BRYANT SINGLEY WALKS into the glass and metal headquarters of the Sarasota Police Department with a shell casing in a surgical glove and heads upstairs to the evidence room. Someone found the brass in a yard and called the police. It's a minor matter, no crime has been reported, but Singley takes his time to get the paperwork right.

He fills out a property report, stows the casing in a plastic bag, seals it, completes an evidence sticker, notes the case number on a paper log and puts the bag in one of the black lockers that line the walls of the room. "In case they need it in another case."

Singley is a veteran of the U.S. Army and the Austin Police Department. He's worked for the SPD for the past eleven years. Today he's doing light duty, hauling a writer around in the passenger seat of his cruiser on what law enforcement calls a ride-along. He gets to fight crime; I get to watch.

Singley's not even out of the building when he gets a call on his radio. I can't hear the assignment, just his summation to me. "We'll clear the call and then it's crossing-guard duty."

The car is black inside with a molded gray plastic backseat with seatbelts and a plastic partition and, in front, a computer mounted on a tray within easy reach of the driver. I squeeze in next to it and we roll.

The first stop is the 1800 block of Loma Linda Street near Sarasota Bay. Two property owners are having an argument over a stolen no trespassing sign. We park on the narrow street with a pest-control vendor on one side and dump trucks rumbling down to the cul-de-sac to excavate for a new home. A woman stands in the driveway.

"Stay by the car until I introduce you. We don't want to scare her," Singley says and walks to the door of a brick and beam house with a metal roof.

After a short conversation, Singley waves me out of the patrol car. He's standing beside a woman in running gear with a bright ball cap pulled over her eyes who says the neighbor in back of her lot keeps taking her sign. She's early fifties with a low, calm voice and a slight curl to her upper lip. She's holding a new sign with a stapler tucked under her arm.

The officer introduces me to the woman—we'll call her Becky. We stand in the sun in the neighbor's driveway and look at the lot, an empty stretch of weeds and that light gray sand that covers most of Florida. In back, a wooden fence gray with age divides the properties. A tall man with a water bottle and T-shirt depicting a sailfish wanders into the conversation. Maybe the husband. The neighbor, a middle-aged woman with broad blond hair and a smile to match, joins the group.

Singley looks at the fence that separates the lot from her neighbor's house and asks for the story. Becky says she knows the neighbor took the sign she'd tacked to the fence but she can't prove it. Singley says, "You two have had some troubles before." He has the advantage of a computer system with a long memory.

Becky think about this revelation. "Yeah," she finally says and accuses the woman in back of tossing her lawn clippings over the fence and wandering into other people's yards. "She's crazy."

Singley doesn't react to the comment. He asks for more details and says he'll be back. Then we climb in the patrol car, drive around the corner to Bahia Vista Street and stop at a wooden house we later learn is 100 years old. A wooden fence surrounds the house, garage and shed. We stand on the gravel landscaping and try the gate. It's locked. The officer and I walk up two concrete strips to the garage and he shouts "Hello?" but no one answers.

We find the woman we'll call Linda around the other side of the house, near a shed. She's mid-sixties, short and thin with dark hair and eyes that bounce between us.

Officer Singley says, "You know why I'm here," and asks if she took the sign. She shakes her head vigorously and says she didn't even know there was a sign and begins to delineate her property lines. She wants to show us the fence so we walk to the back of the house and she points to a tree on her land. Someone has sawed off the limbs that would have hung over the fence. Linda accuses her neighbor of doing that, when she wasn't home.

Singley asks for her name and date of birth and then tells her how it's going to be: she'll agree to keep to her side of the fence and Becky will do the same. "Just ignore each other," he says and we return to the empty lot, where Singley tells the same thing to Becky, who looks up and down the street and shakes her head and frowns.

We sink back into the car and bathe in the air conditioning and head to our next assignment—lunch at Nancy's BBQ, where we sit outside and eat pulled pork sandwiches and talk about the Temptations, Bobby Womack and early Michael Jackson, "Before he fixed his nose," Singley says. How about Etta James? "That's my mama's generation."

I ask him about recent incidents involving police and the use of force, including one that happened a few days ago in Sarasota. He declines to comment, saying "I wasn't there." His philosophy about policing is simple. "I don't comment on what I don't know," then adds, "I just want to go home at the end of the day." Go home alive, he means.

At Southside Elementary School, it is hot and getting hotter, with temperatures and humidity in the upper 80s. It's the kind of day where if you stand outside, you find a patch of shade. In the middle of the crosswalk, there is no shade.

This morning Officer Singley got word that the crossing guard at Southside couldn't work so Singley's lieutenant assigned the duty to him. I can't tell if this is scut work or part of the chief's community policing policy. Probably neither.

We arrive before 2:45 p.m. for a one-hour shift. Singley parks on the grassy shoulder and hits the roof lights to slow traffic. Sometimes it works. Then he climbs out, dons a yellow vest and whistle and waits at the corner of South Osprey and Webber by the signal box for pedestrians. On the rough concrete sidewalk someone has spray painted in perfectly straight letters the words, "Wait here."

We wait.

When the kids show up, Singley's ready. He watches everything—cars going too fast through the school zone, cars parked on the sidewalk in a nearby community, a guy driving with a phone to his ear, a man on a ladder half a block away. One minute he smiles and says hello to parents and children, the next he yells at a young female driver to buckle her seatbelt. He's got eyes in back of his head.

He's also got a cheerful banter going with the people leaving school, and not just the mothers and grandmothers with their younger kids and strollers and umbrellas. He asks the children what grade they're in and why they're carrying a basketball and whether they or their younger sister has more freckles. Then he punches the button on the pole and blows his whistle and walks to the middle of the intersection and wishes them all a good day.

"It's hot," he says on his way back and looks for more pedestrians and punches the button and does it all over again.

At 3:50 p.m. the sidewalk empties and we pile into the squad car and head for headquarters. As we drive on Osprey, something about the black VW Jetta in front of us catches his eye. In the 1600 block of Main Street, Singley calls in the tag number and pulls the car over.

"Wait here," he says.

Approaching the driver's side of the car slowly, he places a palm on the rear window to mark the car in case the driver flees and leans forward to talk. When he gets back in the cruiser he says, "She says she doesn't know why I pulled her over," and punches the license number and tag into the computer. Up comes a photo of the driver's father and a yellow block of type that says the tag has expired. Singley compares the woman's information on the screen with her license and through a series of drop-down menus completes the ticket. He clicks a button labeled "issue citation" and a printer between the seats spits out two copies of what looks like a grocery-store receipt. He gives one copy to the driver.

Then it's back to the glass and metal headquarters and we're done. I thank him for the ride. We shake hands. It's still hot and he's got another hour and a half to go before his twelve-hour shift is up but he smiles anyway.

An uneventful day . . . but at least we both get to go home.

15. BEHIND THE BADGE

WE GATHER ON THE second floor of the Sarasota Police Department to celebrate our graduation. There's a cake, a couple of proud parents and about twenty members of the SPD Citizens' Academy. We're a collection of real estate agents and financial advisers, retirees and writers. We have come to peek into the guarded world of law enforcement and over the past twelve weeks we've learned about the hazards of policing on both sides of the badge.

Members of the SPD command staff are here, Deputy Chief Pat Robinson and the captain of patrol operations, Kevin Stiff, as well as those who organized the academy, Training Officer Jeff Dunn and the volunteers who lugged coolers of soda and water and boxes of pastries and name cards to class every week.

They have certificates, photos and a parting message for us: we've helped them as much as they've helped us.

"We are grateful for people who want to live through our eyes," Capt. Robinson says. "Officers are put under an immense amount of stress. The more folks we can educate on why we do things, the better our interaction with the citizens."

Jeff Dunn says officers also benefit from the class by getting feedback from knowledgeable citizens.

Robinson echoes that, adding that police can become jaded because they deal with a small but difficult portion of the population. "Sometimes you lose perspective." (To attend a future Citizens' Academy, you can download an application at the SPD website.)

For our part, we've learned about legal rights and wrongs, equipment and procedures, prostitution and traffic stops, court cases and crowd control. We've heard from the victim advocate, the public information officer, the state attorney, the coordinator of volunteers. We've watched K-9 dogs attack and officers defend themselves. We've investigated a crime scene, toughed it out in the use-of-force simulator and fired weapons at the gun range.

In between, we've listened to officers describe their background and their passion for the job.

In twelve weeks we've discovered nothing is simple. Most officers play by the rules. Some don't. During traffic stops, most people are polite. Some shoot cops. When we watch video of situations where police use force, the solution looks simple. Hindsight will do that. But we weren't in that battle, with bullets and adrenalin flying, with limited time and information and options. Under pressure, people make decisions that are hard to understand. The second-guessing, the labels *good* and *bad* . . . those come later.

After riding with officers, sharing a meal and listening to their stories, many of us are convinced the most interesting part of the course isn't about guns or self-defense or crime scenes or SWAT. It's about the officers themselves.

Getting them to open up might be the biggest cause for celebration.

ABOUT THE AUTHOR

During his career, Jeff Widmer has worked as a dishwasher, surveyor, guitarist, journalist and marketing professional. He has contributed to *US Airways* and *National Geographic World* magazines, the Sarasota *Herald-Tribune, BIZ 941* and *SRQ Daily*. He has also served as an account executive at several advertising agencies. A native of Pennsylvania, he lives in Sarasota, Florida.

You can connect with Jeff through his author page at Amazon (https://www.amazon.com/author/jeffwidmer), follow him through his website (http://jeffwidmer.com/) or share your comments through his social media presence on Facebook (http://www.facebook.com/jeff.widmer), Twitter (@jrwidmer), LinkedIn (http://www.linkedin.com/in/jeffwidmer) and Pinterest (http://pinterest.com/jrwidmer/).

BOOKS BY JEFF WIDMER

Peak Season: A CW McCoy novel
Riding with the Blues
The Spirit of Swiftwater

Made in the USA
Columbia, SC
23 September 2021